I Am A Hologram From 2046

By Naomi Elizabeth

My, Uh, Innermost Thoughts, Apparently

Contents

Drawings

Hate And Death

Me Being Angry

Philosophy Of Underwear

Pictures Of Naked Ladies

My Whole Thing With Karlheinz Stockhausen

A Study In Revulsion

Obsessions Of A Fuckhead

The Worst Women Ever

Conformity And How Cool It Is

Artifice, Fakeness, And Civilization

The Reasons Why My Project Interests Me

Why Are We Alive

Do You Want To Hear About How Depressed I Am?

What I Think About Music

Living In A Fantasy World

Telling Yourself You Suck – For Success

Not Giving Up - So Many Times In A Row

I Am A Cripple

Cooking Tips: Never Cook Again!

An Essay: Detractors Solely Degrade Themselves

Warning: Not Funny

Warning: This material is not funny. One day I want to write some other volume that's funny, but this one is rude and technical. It mainly serves to reveal the bleakness of my outlook on life, and I don't know if you, personally, are ready for that! I would like to do a different one that's like an easy-reader for assholes on planes. But this one is totally brutal and may scare you.

Who fucking reads a book anyway? Are you retarded? Do you not have streaming video on the Internet? Books are a dollar, I'm pretty sure that means no one gives a crap. You must be on a plane, or in the hospital I guess.

I hate the casual, down-to-earth style of contemporary writing. Everyone has such an easygoing and straightforward air, it's like the author is just your friend, and you're out at a nasty café together, just chatting over a gross beverage. Everyone is so whimsical and fun, it's a nightmare. I hate that, and I hate the fact that history was unable to prepare me for the fact that I WOULD BE WRITING IN THE VERY SAME BARFY STYLE.

Actually, I feel that I should apologize, because my internal monologue is not very feminine or sexy. To me, it sounds like Max Headroom in here. I believe it was Max Headroom who said "Yes, t-t-t-t-tune into Network 23. The network that's a *real* mind-blower [*his head explodes then reappears*] And I love, love, l-l-love... love those blip-blip-blip-blipverts". It doesn't sound exactly like that, but that is a relatively accurate approximation. It's disturbing on a lot of levels. You're probably thinking, "well I used to think this girl was attractive in a way, but now that I'm perusing the contents of her mind, I'm getting the impression she is too much like Max Headroom, and I don't have as much of a boner anymore." Apologies!

Also next time I'm going to write a steamy tell-all where I get f***ed in lots of fancy hotels and I reveal the exact sizes of all the Hollywood A-list wangs. And, it's going to be a searing indictment of the entertainment industry too, and a lot of people are going to lose their jobs because I bring to light their true evils. Additionally I'd like to do a detailed account of which types of underwear I prefer to wear on any given day according to my many fanciful moods (*true). Wait actually I am going to write about that, that is an important topic.

I understand if you are mainly interested in skipping ahead to the parts of the book that have sex in them. I can point you in that direction now to save time, it's no problem. Obviously the chapter titled Men would be where you would want to start. The X Files Lesbian Fan Fiction has some adult content too. My First Internet Porn is sort of misleading, because it implies that I participated in porn, whereas really I was just looking at a porn website for the first time. The part called A Study In Revulsion is sort of sexual, in a way, but mainly regarding serial rapist murderers. I'm not sure if you're into that sort of thing.

Running Over Bicyclists

Today I almost killed some guy on a bike while I was driving, because I didn't see him when I was changing lanes. And I have two suggestions for this guy, because it was an emergency and all and we didn't really have time to talk. First of all, sir, if you only have half a second to get someone's attention, I wouldn't yell "Do you know how to drive???, " because that is a very rhetorical question, a question which is apt to send me farther into my reverie. Honestly even now there is no easy answer to that question, it really makes a person wonder: "What could I do better? Are there rules for driving experts that I am not aware of? What are the secrets of the pros?" And so on. Second of all, I wouldn't scream at me like a little bitch, because it ruins the pathos that I want to feel during a moment when something very serious is happening. The tone of the screaming itself led me to believe that someone would certainly kill him in the near future.

Men

So there is all this information out there about men and how they are touching themselves all the time and how they never have enough sex and it's this whole awful situation. But from a woman's perspective, it's really hard to tell. You are keeping the boners a secret, men! We can't tell they are there! I guess this is one of the great cover-ups of modern times. Anyway it's really working and congratulations everyone.

If there's one thing I have sympathy for, it's that men seem to be going around in a constant state of sexual repression. Women don't have that problem as bad most of the time, but I go out of my way to relate because I can imagine how stupid it would be.

Ok so here's a story that has some boners in it, there's the off chance it could result in you having a boner, I suppose, so I apologize in advance. Hopefully the comedy value will outweigh your troubles in this instance. So I was taking a shower with my boyfriend at the time, and it was very chill, nobody had a boner, we were just hanging out. And then he asked me if it would be ok if he could put some soap on my ass and then kneel down and use the soap to wash his face with. Creative, right? So I said ok that's fine and he did it, and then that gave him a boner and we ended up having sex in the shower.

So after we got out and we were drying off I looked in the mirror and realized I had been wearing a shower cap the whole time, I put it on way before all this other stuff and forgot it was there. And I realized that the whole time we were having sex he must have been looking at this shower cap and he didn't mention it or suggest I take it off! What's up with men? Could I have been wearing a Jack Pumpkin Head on my head? What would I have to be wearing on my head for him not to have a boner anymore?

Then, a separate time, we were watching a documentary on TV about serial killers, and he started touching my breasts. And that's where I personally have to draw the line and say no, because those are two independent emotions that I don't want to experience at the same time.

I also don't want to hear any music while having sex. First of all, it's melodramatic and highly embarrassing. But mainly it's a distraction. When I listen to music I generally try to concentrate on it and hear everything about it, so basically it is a multi-tasking scenario that's been created. Too many things to pay attention to at the same time, for no good reason. Additionally, and this refers mainly to the embarrassment, but I have a tendency to envision that the singer of the band is there in the room with you being uncomfortable while you have sex. Don't make singers have to endure that type of humiliation, if possible. They don't want to think that that's what they've contributed to your life.

Obviously the next question I need to answer is, how often do I take it in the ass? That is something I would definitely do every once in a while, as a favor. I wouldn't do it for myself though, because it's mildly unpleasant, and I would feel relieved when it was over. It's not *that* bad, it's better than filing taxes, for example, but I can't say I ever enjoyed it either. One thing I would like to do, however, at some point, is get f***ed in the ass as a Christmas present to my boyfriend. Then I think I would really enjoy it, as long as it's on Christmas. If you happen to be reading this book, and then one day we end up dating in the future, remind me that I said this should be your Christmas present.

And here's another thing. I don't understand why girls won't give their gentleman friend a blowjob more often. Think of it this way, if some people were trapped in an elevator and all you had to do was push a button and they could get out, why wouldn't you do it? Isn't that inhumane? Wait did my analogy even make sense?

In conclusion of this chapter, I think it would be funny to consider: what if something I had written here chanced to give you a boner, and then you found out I didn't actually write it at all, and it was all ghostwritten by a man! Haha, fooled you, this was all penned by Gary the Dick Man, who has a dick! And now, consequentially, you're gay. Just so you know, it was all written by me and I am in all ways biologically a female, so if you got a boner then everything is cool, but it could have happened!

Bottom Line: Cats

Are you obsessed with cats? When you meet people do you ask them for a complete detailed physical description of their cat? Do you like to call your cat a different name every time you speak with him/her?

I don't really like cats that much, but here is a list of all the names I often call my cat:

Mango Child, Miniature Man, Cat Burger, Hamburger Man, Fatso, The Tiniest Biggest Man, Wigwam, Cat Man, Orangeball, The Bag Man, L'il Megaworm, and Kittyhambur.

When I said that I wasn't that into cats, could you tell I was joking? Could you tell that I was extremely enthusiastic about cats that whole time?

My First Internet Porn

I'll never forget the first time I saw porn on the Internet. The website was called arizonawhores.com. It was a few years back in the day but it still seems like yesterday. I'm trying to look up the site right now, but all I'm getting is "Connecting to arizonawhores.com…". Oh damn it. The connection has timed out. The server at arizonawhores.com is taking too long to respond. Sigh. Anyway let me tell you about this website because it was so special and I'm sure there's never been another one like it before or since! When I looked through the pages, I was regaled with story after story of these incredible men, one of whom was named Spazz, who would always drive around and just happen to find a young woman of Arizona standing outside an office or a restaurant. In each case they would offer her money, put her in their truck, then go to their house and bang her. The tale would always end when the men would decide to forego the monetary aspect of the transaction and send the slut on her way penniless. In the corner of the page it said "The Fuck For Free State".

You might ask, but how could this all be true? I have to say, there is no doubt in my mind that these events all really happened, because there were hundreds of pictures to prove it. Believe me, the veracity of these stories would stand up in any court of law, no question, since the evidence was very very graphic. Every scene was immaculately well lit, and the camera focus was exemplary at all times. There was no dark or blurry corner in any frame of the many adventures of Spazz.

The Troll P.R. Company

If you're going to hire someone to write publicity for you, why not consider hiring a troll? Trolls can spark all sorts of thought provoking debates, and incite enthusiastic responses from everyone they reach out to. Trolls are always available for a healthy argument, and lots of times, they'll tell you something you'd never think of in a million years. Unfortunately, trolls often hide in the dingiest corners of the web, and their insights never come to be appreciated for their true worth. Here are some things that trolls may or may not one day say about me, in the contemplation of my place in the world and the merits I may or may not have achieved.

That voice sounds like a guinea pig being waterboarded.

Naomi takes a wide variety of drugs and has sex with strangers for very little money, possibly even $10.

Naomi is entirely too fat and hideous to meet my standards for a sexual partner.

I would have sex with her, but afterwards I would have to douse my wiener with ethanol.

I would have sex with her, but afterwards I would have to chop off all her limbs and throw her body into five separate rivers.

Naomi Elizabeth is an automaton propelled only by stupidity.

Naomi has little to no talent and cannot execute music properly.

This is setting off my hag radar.

Naomi has concluded that she herself is cool, whereas other people are not, in her mind, as cool.

Whoever listens to this cunt should die in a hole.

Death to Obama supporters, death to liberals, allah hu akbar.

I strongly dislike this "woman" and her trashy "music".

Why listen to such a sorry excuse for music, made by this ugly wench, when you could be enjoying real songs made by talented people, like Arcade Fire? Nope.

Arcade Fire? Fag.

Only fag here is you buddy.

Friday Night Rats

Uh, Naomi, I want to stay home tonight and work on my stupid book, and write about how weird and abusive people are to each other for no reason. No, shitface, it's Friday night. Tonight you are going to go out and see your friends play in a band and act normal and talk to people. I put some of your favorite wine into an empty water bottle, and you're going to put that in your bag and go downtown and walk past the alley looking for rats. Oh, well I do like it when I see the rats.

The next day: Thanks Naomi your advice really worked and I had a great time! I drank the wine out of my bag, and it was partitioned accurately in the water bottle into an amount that would not make me wasted enough to lose my cool. People I knew said funny things that I laughed at, and the band was excellent. I did not, however, see any rats, although I looked extensively. I think the rats know when it's Friday night and they clear the hell out of the way. I'm pretty sure there are only two or three rats living in all of downtown LA anyway. They are so rare, it's almost like seeing a unicorn.

Nazi Scrapbooking Club

Don't you just love to reminisce about old times by looking at historic black and white photos? The grainy shots with worn out edges give everything such a rustic, old-timey look. Even if you were never there, seeing those classic Nazi photos from WWII takes you right back in an instant! The gas chambers in the concentration camps look so quaint and dusty. You feel like you knew personally every one of those folks in that pile of bodies.

The Funniest Word In The World

The funniest word in the world is hamburger. There are a lot of other funny words out there that are also important, such as preemie, for example, but hamburger is the winner. Being an American in Berlin is an incredible experience, because every street and neighborhood there is named after hamburgers. They have Leitzenburger Strasse, Lichtenburger Strasse, Blankenburger Strasse, as well as Frankfurter Allee, and Heinrich-Heine-Strasse. When I went there I was walking around all day laughing. Hamburgers are all around us. I even went to see the minerals and gems at the natural history museum, and there was a crystal in the exhibit called Hambergite. They are a part of our world.

A Luv Letr

Sumtimz u dont evn want 2 spel. Ur liek, "fuk u mom, I don evn care abuot ur stupd crap". Sum peolp cant spel 4 shit n I m startin 2 think they no sumthing we dont. I think they r rite. When I spel bad itz liek da hole world iz made out uv rozez n shit.

Dis reminds me uv sumthing Frank Booth wod say. "U no what a luv leter is? Itz a bulit form a fukin gun, fukr! U raceve a luve letr form me ur fuked forvr! U undersatdn fuk? Il send u stratg 2 hell, fuker!" Me im not 2 much liek Frnak Both. If u git a lov lter form me, it wil porbaly be rilly nise. I m mor uv a nise pernsn.

U no who rilly cant spel 4 shit is da catz on da intemernt. Sum cal dem lol-catz. Is da eductionasl sestem faylin for dese anamalz? We hav cut da bujet 4 cat skoolz 2 muhc! R u lol-ing at there excpenze? Iz not fenny u no, iz a sereace porbalm in da contriy. I m gon strat a cat skool at ma hose. Send all yor litl delinqueze 2 me n I wil

trane them to wirte liek a dick-shonary. Sum1 haz
2 take a stan on dis.

But u no, da hole thgin with dese lol-catz
cold b a cotpsaracy. Mabye dis carp waz not evin
rwiten bi da ctaz in da frists playc. MYABE IT
WUZ RITTWEN BI DOGZ, DID U EVEN
THNIK UV THAT U GUYZ? BUTT... WHY
WOLD DA DOGZ DO SUMETHNIG LIEK
THS?? UV CORTSTE THEIRZ THE
POSTOBOLITE THAT THEY R JEST STUPD.
BUTT... MABE THEY R TRIEYGN 2 MAKE
CATZ LOUK DUM... 2 MAKE THMSEVLZ
LOUK BETER. THNK ABUOTE IT 4 1
SEONEK.

Epic Stories

Let me tell you a little story that happened
a long time ago, one of the epic moments of my
life and many other people's lives. It happened at a
bar we used to frequent because they didn't card
anyone and it was right down the street. I was
there with my sister, my friend Stanley, and some
other best friends forever type friends. At this bar
worked a waitress who was a recent immigrant
from Russia, and as you can try to imagine, she
had a very surly and bitter disposition. Anyway the
bar also served food, and this bitchy waitress was
walking around with a plate of fried mushrooms
that had been ordered by someone named Anna.

Now, I'm not going to say that my friends
ever drank any alcohol or smoked any large
amounts of marijuana. But what I will say is, that
they were, generally speaking, delirious and
ravenous at all times, and this particular day was
no exception. Overall, there was some yelling,
some obnoxiousness, and some hunger. They

proceeded to take the fried mushrooms from the chick, saying "Our friend's name is Anna", having a dim but lucid understanding that Anna had never ordered this food.

Stanley and my sister embarked on an immediate food race to eat this food. It was as if they knew that their time on earth to snack would be extremely limited. They were eating really fast. The waitress soon realized that she had made a huge mistake and served the wrong belligerent jerks. She came back and snatched the plate away, rankled with irritation, and started patrolling back to the kitchen without saying anything. Stanley stood up and yelled after her: "Nuh-uh Fool! That's the baby's lunch!"

This next story is going to require something extra from you. It's going to ask that you draw upon your innate ability to emulate an Indian accent. I'm talking about India here, not Native Americans or anything. I feel confident that you have that secret skill, of saying things with the same voice that an Indian person would use. If you don't think you can handle it, then you will have to hand the book over to someone else who has performance skills, and get them to read the story to you accurately. The choice is yours.

My Indian friend heard this tale from her grandma. Basically one day the tiny Indian grandma was walking with her daughter (my friend's aunt) along the scenic cliffs of La Jolla (the Pacific Ocean). The younger woman chanced to slip on the rocks, and fell into the water. The tiny grandma became distressed upon seeing her progeny in the sea. She put her hands on the sides of her face and yelled over and over, in her Indian accent grandma voice "Dat is my daughter in dee water!"

Here is a series of epic stories centered around the teaching career of my friend Carrie. She has spent tons of time hanging out in public schools with kids who have developmental disabilities, mostly autism. As you can imagine, she has met a lot of characters over several years working in this capacity!

Firstly, she was talking one day with a little student who had high-functioning autism. She was wearing eyeglasses at the time which had an anti-reflective coating over the lenses. During their conversation, the kid said to her, "Miss Carrie, it seems that your glasses contain a portal to the unknown".

Another time, she was hired to watch a group of special ed kids, to assist the teacher during a P.E. class. She was told that: the kids keep trying to climb over the fence and leave the school, so your job is mainly to keep them from climbing the fence. Since she often goes by the name "Miss Carrie" at school, the group had started to call her "Miscarriage". Rude! So how was she able to wrangle these jerks and keep them from leaving the school grounds? Carrie said she would bring in her laptop and let them all play with it and download stuff during the whole class.

Every once in a while, Carrie teaches kids who are so disabled that they can become violent, and can't use language or talk out loud. There was one kid who was completely nonverbal, whose only means of communication was a little box he wore which had buttons on it that he could press to convey basic ideas. She said that when he was overwhelmed and needed to take a break, he would be grabbing onto her hair with one hand, and press the "I need to take a break" button with the other hand. Then he would press a button that would play the "manamana" song by the muppets, over and over, and rock back and forth.

Then there was the kid who made a sign which said "standing is cancelled". He was riding the bus with Carrie, and she asked him to get out of his seat, so that some old people could sit in it. This annoyed him even after the bus ride was over, and led him to make the "standing is cancelled" sign.

One of her best students of all time was another kid who had Asperger's or something, who had his own theory about dolphins and giant squids. He was against dolphins, claiming they were overrated and too showy. He thought the giant squid should be the hero as opposed to the underdog. He would say, "Why does everyone like dolphins? Dolphins can attack humans, you know". He was also opposed to certain items of clothing that he felt were too showy. He was against flip flops for example. He would say "Do I have to let people wearing spaghetti straps into my house?" During his history class, he was learning some facts about King George. Then he would go around saying "King George is a bastard" all the time.

This isn't really an epic story. It's more of a tiny story, which should nonetheless be related in the interest of preserving it for future generations. Stanley, who we remember as the Baby's Lunch friend, used to have a dog named Bjork (RIP), who would sometimes sleep out in a kennel in the back yard. At one point it was discovered that a mouse was living in the kennel too. Eventually the mouse died and its body turned up over in the corner, a week later. The dead mouse and the dog were roomies!

Oh, actually, this is now reminding me of the story of Adria Hempbum. In college Stanley had a roommate who turned out to be a terrible loser, since he skipped out on the rent and wouldn't pay hundreds of dollars that he owed. Of course after that happened, all the possessions in this person's room became the property of Stanley and the other inhabitants of the apartment. One day, some friends and I came over and gathered around on the floor, to look inside the real prize of the collection, which was the guy's personal diary.

Now incidentally, this guy was an outright, flaming homosexual. His journal was full of gay thoughts and half-baked ideas for fashion designs. But that fact was a foregone conclusion, as all of this was happening at San Francisco State, and all my friends were gay then and are gay now. The gayness was not any part of why this was amazing.

The reason why this diary was amazing is because the dude was a total moron who couldn't spell or draw. His fashion design sketches were *literally* stick figures, with squiggles for hair and smiley faces for faces. A lot of them were composed of only 5 or 6 haphazard wavy lines. These idiotic scribbles were supposed to represent brilliant flashes of haute couture women's wear glamour. In his mind they were the finest eveningwear! There was one drawing in particular, the most elemental squiggle of all, and the caption for this was "Adria Hempbum".

fashion
design
sketch
→

"Adria Hempbum"

I don't know if this next story could accurately be described as epic, but it is about an event that was at least completely weird. This is the story of the weirdest surprise party for someone's birthday possibly ever. It started out normally, a bunch of friends of Bill, the birthday person, showed up at a friend's apartment early, before he arrived. When we got the text that he was on his way, we were told that we would all be ushered into the bathroom and then later we would emerge and that would be the surprise. Everything seemed standard and manageable up to this point.

So we herded ourselves into the bathroom. There were 16 of us in there. Nobody could fit in the bath tub because it was full of balloons. The theme of the party was "Billoons" in honor of Bill. There were also billoons hanging from the ceiling as well, filling in every empty molecule of space above our heads. To give you an idea of how crowded it was, the girl standing next to me couldn't even put both feet on the ground, she was standing on one leg. I realized this and pointed her in the direction of an empty square of the floor next to my foot. We literally could not have fit even one more person in this bathroom.

After several minutes of waiting, the truly bizarre element of this party came to light. Bill's girlfriend intended for us to wait in there until he had to pee, and then we were to jump out and yell surprise when he was trying to get in the bathroom. We started to understand that we were incarcerated for an indefinite period. Bill arrived at the house and could be heard laughing outside with the hosts. It started to get hotter and hotter in the bathroom. No air was circulating. Also, the light was turned off and night was falling outside. It got darker and darker. We all began sweating and whispering and complaining.

People started counting the minutes and sending out desperate text messages with their phones in airplane mode. 15 minutes passed, 20 minutes. People were meeting each other for the first time and introducing themselves. The air was gross and breathy. I probably smelled like a worker in a shipyard. At first there were comparisons brought up to a crowded subway, and then as more time elapsed, the comparisons turned to the holocaust. We considered mutiny. I took off my sweater and tried to fan everyone with a feeble piece of paper that was in my bag.

A text came in that the girlfriend had been giving Bill lots to drink in order to expedite the process of our liberation. Finally, he came in after 33 minutes! We yelled surprise and emerged sweaty and confused. He was confused as well, and he apologized over and over for being the source of so much human torment.

The other cool thing about this party was that the hosts owned a cat with a Hitler moustache, AND a pet snake with a Hitler moustache! They claimed it was just a coincidence.

X-Files Lesbian Fan Fiction

You know what's the most amazing invention in the world is fan fiction. I wish I had 500,000 extra hours to live, so I could read every one of these stupid stories. I feel like I *need* to write something extra lame, and it has to be as lame as possible, it has to be unforgivably stupid...

I woke up in an unfamiliar room. The first thing I saw was a nondescript white ceiling, and featureless white walls as I started to look around me. There was a grey office sofa with woven upholstery, that looked like it was starting to age. There was a door that was shut, and no windows at all. I was lying face up on a metal hospital stretcher. White sheets were draped over me, but I could still feel the coldness of the metal underneath.

I lay motionless. I was trying to remember what had happened to me the night before, but I drew a blank. My heart started to race, as I tried harder and harder to recall anything in my recent past or make any mental connection to this empty sterile room.

I wondered if I might be hurt somehow. I sat up and pulled the sheet off of me. I felt normal, maybe a little dizzy. My arms and legs moved normally as I looked down at my body. I was wearing only a bra and panties.

I still knew who I was, I was Melissa Fields. I had recently gotten a temp job in a new biotech office in my neighborhood. I didn't know exactly what they were working on, they wanted to keep all the technical details a secret. I was happy to stick to the secretarial end of the business. I could remember parking my car in the lot on Monday morning, but that was the last thing... And when was Monday? It seemed that almost any amount of time could have passed since then...

I thought about the possibility of opening that door, and my heart started to race even more. I was in my underwear, what would I do once I got outside? Should I wrap the sheet over myself and try to run? Should I scream or make a sound? Turning over all these questions, I started to shake a little bit, and I was getting close to a point where I might cry.

All of a sudden there was a knock on the door, and a beautiful woman walked in. She had red hair that was swept to the side, pale skin, and blue eyes. She wore a navy blazer and pant suit. She looked at me with a sincere gaze, as though she wanted to answer all the questions that were running through my mind. "Hello, Melissa, my name is Agent Dana Scully", she said, closing the door behind her. "You've been through so much, but it's over now, everything is OK".

I didn't know what to say, and I just started to cry, sitting there on the side of the stretcher. Agent Scully sat down next to me and put her arms around me. She held me tightly as she was saying, "Melissa we know everything. Those people can't hurt you anymore."

Through my tears I finally managed to say, "How do you know me? How do you know my name? Where am I?" I told her how I had just woken up right now, not remembering anything since Monday morning.

Scully stopped for a moment and looked at me. She pulled my long dark hair back from my face and held it in her hands with concern. "You really don't remember anything that happened to you?"

When I looked back at her with a blank stare, she knew that she would have to tell me everything. "We have been investigating the Altalogic company where you worked for months", she began. "The office that opened in your town was new, but they had been developing experimental medications under other names for a long time. Their specialty was a new class of anesthesia drugs, and we believe that the drugs had strange properties. We aren't sure, but it seems that they were designed to clear away the conscious mind of the user, leaving an empty space so that the body could be inhabited by another being. As they grew closer to achieving that aim, they became more and more covert about their laboratory practices. They started to reject funding, and instead they started to receive donations from a private anonymous source. The documentation of their research all but disappeared.

"We found out that you were hired by this company to serve as a test subject, to have your identity erased, and to leave your body behind as a shell for a non-human entity to join into. We were able to raid the building a week ago, on the suspicion of your disappearance, and found you there unconscious, attached to an intricate system of intravenous chemicals."

It was too much for my brain to process at once. How long had I been knocked out in that place? What had they done to me while I was there? I couldn't think anymore. I couldn't take it anymore. All of a sudden, I didn't care. I realized that Agent Scully had her arms around me, had both of her hands in my hair. I looked up at her and suddenly I kissed her. I still don't know why.

Outer Spac⸺

Oh⸺
behind war⸺
so you can
fishbowl or⸺
connector t⸺
atmospher⸺
very speedy⸺
out there yo⸺
say "Oh no

Ho⸺
want to go ⸺
infinitely pa⸺
Doesn't eve⸺
as hell and t⸺
sounds like
You're stuc⸺
all eternity, ⸺
stay in your⸺
variety you ⸺
cylindrical b⸺

riveting, I can't wait to be trapped in here for-fucking-ever. Thanks, space!

Why are spaceships always designed like huge minivans? The tinted, ergonomic glass gives them the ambience of a dustbuster, and you will be the hamster that is entombed within. And you know that the spaceship air system has to suck. You know it will be like the worst dried-up airplane air, blowing its dry and germy storm all over you. You know you're going to be glaring at the vent all day, trying not to breathe.

You guys, wake up. Fuck space.

"Naomi, wtf?"

Voices are heard saying "Uh, why is this chick getting all mad about space? I don't know, but she's really freaking out."

Furthermore, is it necessary for spaceships to always have these metal swishing hydraulic doors that open automatically and go inside the wall? Swishing and swishing, don't they have those doors at the mall? Number one, that technology has to be already twenty years old, at least. Number two, how is it even contributing to anything to have those doors? Where are they even appropriate? In my opinion those could only be useful in top secret science laboratories under the ground, where mad scientists try to re-animate severed human heads and take over the world.

It's gross, I'm telling you, space is gross. Everyone wears unitards. How could that be the future? What if you have to pee? What if you forgot your favorite MP3s at home? You know there isn't going to be a wifi spot in outer space, you're not going to be able to read blogs. And you're going to be trapped on board with a lot of scientists, good luck getting them to entertain you for the remainder of your existence.

"Is she done? Do you think she is going to say more stuff about space? I don't know, what should we do? Let's keep quiet, maybe she will stop by herself."

The Mask: 1994 – 2011

I want you to know that I'm putting a lot of work into writing this. Not just time spent ironing out the syntax, but also hours of research. I decided it's in all of our best interest if I watch the 1994 film The Mask starring Jim Carrey and Cameron Diaz, and put together a thorough retrospective for you. What did we miss the first time that we really need to know? How are the catchphrases holding up after all these years?

Are you ready to go on a cinematographic journey with me? I'm already wincing a lot and I haven't even started yet. But I hereby promise to see the whole thing, even if I have to take breaks, ---because I love you---.

Oh my god The Mask is so bad I don't think I can sit through this. Why am I doing this? OK for the readers. Think of the readers, they need to know. Focus.

Well look at you. Look who's too cool for The Mask. You stupid bitch. Sit still and enjoy it, or I'll make you watch it twice! This is for science!

12 minutes: So far I'm doing ok. Everything's chill. A tube killed this one guy who was underwater, and then this other guy is going to rob the bank. Not sure yet what I'm supposed to learn.

17 minutes: Is this what it feels like to be 7 years old?

19 minutes: Ok it just became exponentially more embarrassing. All this fucked up shit just happened. Can't explain. He said "Smokin'" but it didn't even matter because so many things were going on. I am hoping there is no one around who can hear me watching this right now. That possibility makes me think I might be blushing.

22 minutes: I accept that this is happening to me. I accept that this is, for some as yet unknown reason, the best possible use of my time on the earth.

31 minutes: Edge City has a serious mafia presence. I'm concerned.

32 minutes: Tasmanian devil pillow on couch

38 minutes: Was jazz music big in the 90s? Did people enjoy living in the 90s?

55 minutes: Wishing someone would call and rescue me, and also that I would get amnesia about promising to finish this.

57 minutes: They searched him and he had a picture of the officer's wife in his pocket! Funyuns

59 minutes: Jim Carrey is actually a talented dancer… Is that what I'm supposed to learn?

62 minutes: Oh yeah, the newspaper bitch who sells him out, I remember that

64 minutes: Getting worried, shit is getting pure evil

76 minutes: Are we friends, do you think? I feel like we get along really well. Hm.

83 minutes: Dog wears mask

86 minutes: Mask diffuses bomb by eating it 6 seconds before detonation

Well it ended. My life feels the same. Maybe all the meaningful lessons are hidden in Son of the Mask. If I really loved you, I would watch that right now. But I'm not making any promises, as that is going to be extremely difficult for me! We will continue this conversation after you calm down…

Uh oh, fools, Son Of The Mask is on, I'm back! No no no no no no no no no no no. Oh yes. It's the next day after that whole debacle with the first Mask, and I'm feeling stronger, ready to handle more than ever.

(For those who don't know, which is everyone, which is as it should be, here is a brief synopsis of Son Of The Mask. Jamie Kennedy is some guy, he puts on the mask and then bangs his wife. She gets pregnant with a demonic prank baby which is like a CGI cartoon dancing baby that does lots of antics. Alan Cumming is the bad guy who is like a Norse god going to earth to ruin things via computer generated follies and bloopers.)

I'm not ready. But I'm doing this for you. Does this prove to you how much I care?

1 minute: Back in Edge City. Kind of excited.

4 minutes: This is so gay.

12 minutes: Alan Cumming what are you doing with your life? You need an intervention man. Your IMDB is like a minefield of pure humiliation.

14 minutes: Please send help.

17 minutes: I do love it when people say "my bad". Note to self: try to say "my bad" more often in life.

18 minutes: By the time you read this, I will be gone.

19 minutes: I want to party with all 10 of the junior high school students who actually watched this.

20 minutes: I had to pause the film. My eyes are bleeding.

23 minutes: Bitch got pregnant when she was banging the green man.

29 minutes: Alan Cumming is the only good part of this movie. His existence is guiding me, lo as I walk through the valley of the shadow of garbage. I take back everything bad I said about you! When there was only one set of footprints, it was then that you carried me! Thanks bro!

36 minutes: "Timmy Tyler, are you my mask baby?"

39 minutes: Does my life suck? Is this what it means to suck?

45 minutes: What are you trying to do to me? Are you trying to break me down? Because it's working! I'm at the end of my rope now and I can't take it anymore! I'm stopping right now. Son Of The Mask is the worst thing that's happened to me in so long! We need to not talk about this for a while, is that ok? I have to decompress.

Epilogue, five years later: I did eventually recover from my experience watching Son Of The Mask, very gradually, and I learned to walk and talk all over again. Feeling much better all around. Haven't gotten my health together sufficiently enough to go back and finish the film yet, although my therapist says it would be good for me. Still don't know how it ends. We can get through this, together.

Comedy Jokes

Don't you love to talk about funny jokes and comedy? Is there anything better than CLASSIC comedy situations?

A First Date: What are some of the things you should classically NOT say when you're on a classic comedy joke first date? Because you know it is so awkward and if you say something crazy you could ruin the whole date!!

1. Which college do you think our kids should go to?

2. Do you think the media keeps insisting that the holocaust really happened because it's run by liberal Jewish communists?

3. If my cat could talk, I bet she would love to call you dad.

4. I used to work as a private investigator… just because I wanted to make sure my ex wife was getting home safe every night.

5. Generally speaking, I only enjoy sex when it's with two black guys at the same time, but maybe you could do an alright job.

6. So what's your annual income?

7. I want you to meet my parole officer.

Inventions of the future: You know what else is funny? Those crazy inventions of the future that we can only DREAM of! What will they come up with next, right guys??

1. In the future they should invent a regular vacuum cleaner that has a giant ball at the bottom instead of a hinge.

2. Instead of sending a birthday card in the mail, what if one would just magically show up in your email inbox? Then it would never get lost!

3. Since it's so hard to read women, what if they could invent shorts that say "Pink" written on the back, so you would know whether their ass was pink?

4. Also, what if there was a way girls could wear little angel or devil wings on their back, so you would know if they are insane?

Jokes about other jokes: Did you ever hear a joke that was so funny, you laughed?

1. I have to see a man about a horse. He has a horse that I really like, so I should go see him and talk to him about that.

2. Oh hey I can't talk right now, I have to catch a time machine back to 2005, because they called and said they wanted my Ugg Boots back, and that it was very important and that I should leave right away.

Drawings

I love drawing, I used to do it all the time, it used to be my "thing". Here are some recent drawings I made!

This one is self-explanatory.

Here's one that's a searing indictment of birds... Or possibly it's a searing indictment of people who don't know what searing indictment means... Oh wait, the joke is on you - morons run the world.

It's not really a searing indictment of birds. I just thought it might be funny, in a not-that-funny sort of a way.

Here's a portrait of some cats I used to live with, enjoying themselves in a fictional setting. Pet portraiture never gets old!

This drawing is about clams.

Small Clams
Court

Hate And Death

Here's where the tone of the book gets really negative and bleak! Maybe I should reserve all my opinions about life until the last day, then I would be able to say for sure whether or not it was all worth it. That's when you should see if I say: yeah that was pretty cool, or else: that sucked and was a complete waste of time as I originally suspected. I should write two versions of a book and then everyone can throw away one version after the final conclusion has been drawn. At this point, it seems like life has the potential to be a giant drag, and the best strategy is to fill it up with trifles and distractions and act as inane as possible at all times.

If life has handed you a raw deal in any respect, you should probably be angry about it. I am so mad that my life isn't perfect. And even if it does turn out that I get every single retarded thing I want in the end, I'll STILL be mad that I had to work all hard while years and years were passing not being perfect.

I have to tell you, it's interesting because every day I make a consistent effort to be as upbeat as possible, but then when I write, I feel like I'm addressing someone who has an overly barren, almost suicidal outlook on life. I feel like reading books is the realm of those who are in the throes of an existential life breakdown. Most of the books I ever enjoyed were first person narratives with protagonists who could barely keep it together. Stringing together barely enough sanity to make it through a day is my bag, apparently.

Maybe I judge the integrity of an individual by that measure too. Being in an extremely dark position in life and then finding a way out of it is a characteristic of a lot of people I identify with. Everyone else just seems like a lightweight. However it bugs me when people consider that human pain and suffering has to be the hallmark of great art. I don't agree with that. Canonizing whatever crippling pain was foisted on you by making it the focus of your projects seems very limiting. Of course all that should be in there somewhere, or even a lot, but not to the degree of being the singular focus.

Me Being Angry

Disclaimer: Although it seems that I am making disparaging remarks about certain parties in this upcoming passage, I want you to know it is only for purposes of comedy and I love everyone. I have no malice and I think we are all doing great! If it seems like I'm actually mad, don't take it personally. You probably just interrupted me trying to die or something.

It's sometimes a reflex to think to yourself "Jesus why are all these people such fucktards?" It's an interesting phenomenon, when you feel that you are surrounded by tools and there's no escape. It could happen to anyone. It's better not to be fueled by anger, if you can avoid it, but every once in a while it won't go away.

So you're consumed by annoyance with these idiots, and then you stop to think for 2 seconds longer and you realize, no, actually the persons in question are reasonably alert. Most people in the world are 90% functional and alert, but then it's that last infuriating 10% that makes you want to run away to a nonprofit cat sanctuary.

But then, having realized that, you begin to understand that you yourself are on some level necessarily causing fury in others. Out there right now, I know for a fact, are many who consider me an abject moron. Even if they took a moment to examine my finer points, like my decent ability to craft lengthy paragraphs, for example, the thought of me makes them cringe in horror.

Unfortunately, even though I am aware of this problem, there's very little I can do about it. Of course I would love to be the person who no one was annoyed by. But no matter how much I try to conduct myself like an adult, the obnoxiousness will seep out of me and fester on someone's nerves until the end of time. Can I even truly apologize for that?

Here is the problem: the problem is that you are the only person who can serve as the default center of the universe for your mental sphere, and as such you are forced in a way to unconsciously compare other people's choices to your own. We can't help it, but we think other people should turn out just the same as us. A lot of us would transfer that power to Steve Jobs if it were possible to do so. We could collectively figure out ways for us all to be more like Steve Jobs.

You would think that was a power reserved specifically for dads. Only dads should have thoughts about making each citizen think the way they do. But noooo. Even a total fuck up like me has those thoughts! And when you're a weird person like me, this thinking doesn't even make any sense, can you imagine me internally dishing out tips and advice to someone on the street, to make them be more "right"?? Does being right mean being more like me?? Um, but seriously, in what universe.

In my experience, I seem to be offensive mainly to sad fatsos who can't get a date. Although maybe that's the demographic sending out the most per capita hatred for everyone. Which is interesting to me because those types don't bother me at all. If anything I'm more engaged by alienated slobs than by a lot of square folks. Whereas the people who bug me the most are these New York/LA success chaser jerks who are SO proud of themselves and consider themselves incredible hotshots, even though they aren't making any money or doing anything interesting. Those guys and gals bug the nuts off of me, pardon my French.

Changing the topic slightly, I want to tell you about how all the people I know including myself are these extreme, die-hard 100% mega-hipsters. Like there's absolutely no doubt about it, no grey area, just straight up hipsters. However, let me tell you a little secret about hipsters. The thing about it is, is that ---hipsters don't know they are hipsters---. In the mind of the person is only the thought "I am a true individual, and I will be universally perceived as such". When in fact all along they are falling into some classic pattern of hipster style and not realizing it. Additionally, the same person could see an unknown hipster walking down the street and say "Look at that filthy hipster jerkoff walking down the street". I don't know if there's a term for this sort of selective blindness, but there should be!

I'm not saying it's bad to be a hipster. More often than not the ethos is accompanied by a sincere and conscientious socio-political agenda, and that's always heartwarming.

You know what makes everyone such giant gaylords is that they have no sense of humor. Or maybe they have one, but it's all feeble and withered from disuse. You know who has no sense of humor is hippies. They are so bad at saying something funny. They should stick to making food that doesn't harm anyone's feelings, which is their main skill set.

And the worst are the indie rock hippie pitchfork crowd. Those people are so repulsed by me, but what they don't realize is that I secretly am one of them who defected. I mean how many acoustic folk rock bands can you actually listen to?

Doesn't it make you have to take a nap after 10 minutes? When you think back to the 60s and Woodstock and all that crap, were those people awesome hipsters? No, they were all raunchy burnouts! Have you ever met someone after they've done 200 hits of acid? It's not a good scene.

And the weird thing about it is, I don't think there's a whole lot of life wisdom cruising around in these circles either. I think a lot of those people are just scraping by emotionally, subsisting on some rotten insubstantial level of spiritual fulfillment. That's what I don't want for my life!

On a separate note, I always think it's weird when people get carried away by the luminaries of 60s literature. Not to discredit the value of their work, but it all seems tainted by this crusty attitude that in my mind characterizes those times. I feel like I'm the only person who is aware of this crustiness enough to have an aversion to it. It's like when you're hanging out with bums downtown, and they're all baked in the sun and brown, until they have a real crust all over them, and they're "done". I feel like all those books are overcooked and toasty and I can't really handle it.

My philosophy of life is sometimes largely based on anger. And all the people I was angry at, I really should have been mad at myself instead, for ever paying attention to them or giving credit to them in the first place. Looking to a bunch of chumps for the answers to existence is going to be a letdown, and I should have seen that all along!

Philosophy Of Underwear

I believe that my underwear choice for any given day is extremely important and needs to reflect the state of my psyche on that day. Allow me to delineate for you exactly what this means for me.

First of all, I can't wear panties that fit badly or are unattractive. That is the baseline of the whole theory, and is true for every day of the week. However, depending on certain factors of mood and circumstance, I could choose something hotter, or more functional, as needed. The first question is, what are my chances of having sex on that day? Obviously, for a day with higher potential, the undergarment will be sluttier. On the opposite end of the spectrum, if I've got my period then the color has to be black and the aesthetics are slightly less of a consideration.

Sometimes, even if I'm relatively certain I will not get laid, I really want to wear something great down there, for the purpose of creating a positive vibe. That has more to do with verve and lightheartedness, than any sort of sexual factor. If you've never tried boosting your mood via lingerie, you might want to consider it. It might just make you amped and give you the power you need to excel. That's a tip you're unlikely to acquire reading motivational business blogs.

But here is a problem I have, and this is a huge problem for me. I can never coordinate the bra and panties I'm wearing to match each other. The thing about it is, if your bra doesn't fit correctly, then it's going to result in a lot of physical pain for you and put a serious dent in your net happiness. The chance of finding a good bra for every day of the week is slim to none. Bras are also tricky since they show under your shirt sometimes, and if you're wearing one that's all lacy and covered with bows and stuff, it might look crappy inside your clothes. All the lace might poke out in a 3D fashion the way aliens would look if they inhabited your body.

So if I locate a good bra, I have to wear it for like a week without changing it, and I can't wash it more often than that, because the fabric would start to get ruined in the laundry. In contrast to the panties which as we all know are only good for a day LBH. The result of all this is that the bra and panties are always on two separate tracks, and it's going to be rare for me to synch them up unless it's truly a special occasion.

Pictures Of Naked Ladies

Sometimes I like to dress myself up like a naked woman and take pictures of myself. I always enjoyed looking at photos of naked ladies anyway, and I always get ideas in my mind for things that I think might hopefully turn out appealing. It's a fun hobby. I used to enlist my girlfriends to help me by asking them to take the actual photos, because when I started I didn't understand the technical aspects of photography or have my own camera. But then I figured out the basic manual settings which was, in the end, pretty straightforward, and now I do it all by myself.

When I'm taking pictures it never enters my mind to wonder how other people will react to them. I don't see it as overtly sexual. I'm definitely not trying to seduce anyone. I don't think I would ever want to do anything that could be categorized as porn, by today's standards.

Most of the time when I'm planning out a photo, my objective is to make it look like some anonymous lady, being photographed by some arbitrary photographer. Ideally the lady would be hot and the photographer would be classy and proficient. It's not about my personality in any special way. I enjoy images that are generic. But generic doesn't mean mediocre in this context, because I hope that the results will be well done. When I say generic I mean that the picture should be exactly what the observer would have expected to see.

One time I took a picture of myself wearing studio headphones, as an example. This wasn't supposed to be a sexy one at all, it was more of a musician's promotional shot. I had clothes on! Anyway, it was funny to me, because a musician –should- be wearing headphones and –should- be looking very sincere while recording something very important. I personally don't give a flip one way or the other about headphones or about looking sincere. But I thought it would be a good photo, because the observer would immediately take it for granted. They would think, "Of course… it's a sincere musician jamming out in a recording studio, this gal must be very talented", while in truth I am off in the distance laughing because I fooled them. Not that anyone should particularly care about that picture. I just wanted to do it for fun.

My Whole Thing With Karlheinz Stockhausen

My whole project and everything that I'm
working on is based on this one quote by
Karlheinz Stockhausen, who was a 20th century
avant garde classical musician. When he said it,
everyone got mad, because it SOUNDS like he is
saying that 9/11 was *freakin cool*, which is rude, and
I don't think that's what he meant. I mean it was
probably translated from German, I don't know,
who knows what German people are ever saying.
Anyway what it means to me is, that artists are
miniscule and useless, when you compare them to
the enormity of world events.

Here's what he said, I took this from
youtube though, so this isn't the original source
material:

'What has happened is - now you all have
to turn your brains around - the greatest work of
art there has ever been. That minds could achieve
something in one act, which we in music cannot
even dream of, that people rehearse like crazy for

ten years, totally fanatically for one concert, and then die. This is the greatest possible work of art in the entire cosmos. Imagine what happened there. There are people who are so concentrated on one performance, and then 5000 people are chased into the Afterlife, in one moment. This I could not do. Compared to this, we are nothing as composers... Imagine this, that I could create a work of art now and you all were not only surprised, but you would fall down immediately, you would be dead and you would be reborn, because it is simply too insane. Some artists also try to cross the boundaries of what could ever be possible or imagined, to wake us up, to open another world for us.'
Karlheinz Stockhausen, Hamburg, September 2001.

To me he was saying that the act of 9/11 was immense in a way that art could never be immense. An artist could never create something which would cause thousands of people to instantly disappear. In effect, real life in this case outweighs art by being more profound and more powerful.

I think what we often forget is, that just being born and being alive in this time and place, is our free ticket to the biggest freakshow ever. I think that the mainstream information we are getting via the news and entertainment, is more surreal and bizarre than the most shocking music performance or art installation or whatever that you've ever seen. The forces of contemporary survival and the animalistic nature of crowd mentality have turned the human race into a bizarre carnival. To me that is what is worth remarking on, and seems to be the only worthy subject matter for an artist in this century.

A couple people have said to me in the past, well if you want to be extreme then why don't you get involved with bondage porn or fetish porn or something like that, which verges on being unacceptable or offensive. But what I wish those people would realize is that "normal" culture is just as screwed up if not more screwed up, than whatever niche of perversion you happen to be shocked by. Civilization has evolved to become completely raw.

Art is a boundary that you draw around a small subset of life. Once it's been isolated its limits become evident. That's why reality will always be more powerful, because times move very quickly these days, important moments are being educed every day, it's hard to even keep up or retain any of it over time. The best a person can hope for as an artist is to have as broad a scope as possible, and try to net as much of reality as possible before setting it down in concrete form.

A Study In Revulsion

Just a note: In this chapter I bring up topics that include racism, violence against women, and human slaughter. I want it to be known that these ideas are presented for artistic purposes only. I am peaceful and friendly and I don't believe that anyone should be subjected to those types of situations. The concepts of anger and rage should be viewed from a distance, as an impartial observer!

I'm here to talk about one of the most offensive and disturbing divergences of music history that mankind has ever known. Power Electronics is the name given to this obscure offshoot of noise and industrial music, and if anyone were paying the slightest attention, it would be absolutely reviled. Not very many people are ever going to know about this music, but a small group of total fuck ups including myself love it and can't live without it.

So what exactly is power electronics? First imagine the sound of a lawnmower or a blender, or the buzzing from a fluorescent light amplified a thousand times. Then imagine that there are no other instruments at all, not even one single note, no melody, no rhythm, no pattern or repetition, ever. All you get is one scary overdriven square wave type thing. Then imagine on top of that the sound of a man's voice, screaming about raping and dissecting innocent people. Voila!

One of the most classic albums of the genre is by Deathpile, made by Jonathan Canady, a first person account of the thoughts of the Green River Killer as he was abducting, raping, and brutally murdering dozens of women. The record is called GR and it's really, really, really-really dark and intense. Here is an excerpt from the lyrics:

"Disgusting fucking whores

Are trash

They're to be used

And thrown away

…They need to be cleaned off the streets

… Whores deserve to have their bodies broken

Whores deserve to have their breath choked out of them

I wish I could choke every last whore"

Why does this appeal to me? Primarily, the composition is so spare and atonal, that it elevates itself to a level similar to some 20th century classical and avant garde music. The simplicity of omitting the "music" from your music is an acquired taste but can be very edifying. And secondly, the brutality and rawness of the vocals are a slap in the face to every other genre of music that I know of. I think of it the way that punk rock must have sounded extreme back in the 70s. Nowadays we're used to punk bands, and they sound relatively mild, but at the time when they were new, I bet they were interesting to hear. For me, it's greater to hear something that shreds and destroys all my preconceptions about how music is "supposed" to sound, than to be comfortable and bored listening to auditory paradigms I'm already familiar with. Once you've heard you favorite bands a thousand times, the material starts to get old. It's time to raise the stakes on your own sense of appreciation!

But doesn't the evil and darkness bring me down? No, I just find it all delightful as an aesthetic demonstration. The bleakness of the tone is more of a color to me than a serious source of pain.

On to the topic of Brethren. The album Savage Inequalities has had a strong influence on me, I've never heard anything like it. I don't know the name of the artist who made it. The only way to describe this record, is as white power terrorist music. It advocates genocide against minorities and gay people, and throws around a little misogyny on the side. It is SO brutal. Let me capture some of these lyrics for you, so you can grow to enjoy them as I have:

> "Put a bullet in that man's head
>
> That man will pillage our land
>
> Take our jobs
>
> And rape our women
>
> Put a bullet in that woman's head
>
> That woman will bring filth, disease, and sickness
>
> Put a bullet in that child's head
>
> That child
>
> Like father like daughter, like father like son
>
> Fire your gun"

What?? Is my sense of humor totally fucked?? I don't think I can honestly explain why this record is so good. I'm not racist, as far as I know. I just think it's incredible that a human made this, and it makes me want to celebrate.

Now we need to talk about
Bloodyminded and about how Mark Solotroff is
an absolute genius when it comes to lyrics and
delivery. Wow!

"Going down to Chinatown to see what's
for sale

Small animals hang in windows

Fowl and hog

Skinned and cleaned

Skinned and cleaned

But I need more

I want you

A whole animal

Hanging from a hook

Skinned and cleaned

Skinned and cleaned by me"

I just don't know what to even say, but
I'm so impressed. I wish you could hear how good
this crap sounds. You wouldn't like it though, it's
awful. It's every bit as offensive as you would
imagine. You should just take it from me that I
fucking love Mark Solotroff and that this chap is
poetry in motion.

So anyway, what's it like to go to a Power Electronics show? First of all, there aren't going to be too many people there. The fans are few and far between, and most of them are solitary ponytail type guys. There are definitely girls who are interested in P.E. also, but to be honest you're likely to see a lot of man-ponytails and beards. I don't know what it is about me in particular, but I seem to be drawn to subcultures that are predominantly composed of antisocial ponytail/beard guys.

Anyway, everyone there will be best friends. It's a unifying choice of entertainment. It will probably all take place at an art gallery or at someone's house. When the performer goes onstage, he or she will most likely stand behind a card table covered with guitar pedals, mixers, cassette players, and maybe some drum machines or keyboards, all connected to each other with different guitar cables. The audience crowds around, holding beers. Sometimes they could push each other or get violent, but sometimes it's peaceful. They stand so close to the table of equipment that they might knock it over or run into the performer. Maybe three to five different acts will go on stage in an evening, with spaces in between for everyone to talk awkwardly. At the end of the night, after talking with all of one's best show friends, one leaves the venue and goes home, having the sense that something of extreme importance has taken place.

Obsessions Of A Fuckhead

Did you ever get so obsessed with something that was incredibly stupid, to the extent that you couldn't justify it to anyone and you knew the whole time that it was making you look like a fuckhead? That basically describes my experience in life for a lot of reasons. But even if no one will ever understand, you can't stop liking the things that you like. Even if every single person you know views you as an obnoxious caricature of a human, you won't be able to turn your back on the lame fancies you have developed. It's just sad but true, no one will get it, and you will be dumb in their eyes.

I have this problem all the time, and particularly regarding my interest in Disneyland, an institution which dominates my existence almost against my will. Even if I say, "The engineering at Disneyland is immaculate and they have laid out the experience of a waking dream there for you, and the attention to detail transports you into a transcendent state where you will realize clearly how life should always be", all anyone would actually hear from me is "Euhh, it was fun, I went there, weeaah" uttered like a retarded person.

It leads me to ask myself, is this a sure sign that I'm a gaylord? Is this the way life is trying to show me the truth about myself, and being a gaylord? But then I always answer, no of course not, the truth is that I love it when robotic animals sing for me and tell me stories. I also enjoy hurtling around at high speeds strapped into a miniature train on a metal track. Who wouldn't love that?

The whole concept of "taking a person seriously" is sort of a rough topic. Even if you respect and admire someone and appreciate all their work, you can still make fun of them or criticize the one thing they did that was substandard. For example, Werner Herzog is probably one of the best people alive in the whole world, but it's too easy to make fun of his accent. It's so dark and German and disturbing. When he says "It's as though the birds in the jungle are not singing, but they are -screaming een pain-", how can you not keep saying that to yourself as a joke throughout the day?

You can't be on the same page as anyone. I can tell that a lot of my peers, whereas they consider me a decent and friendly individual, don't take me seriously at all as an artist. Partially because I don't act "serious" or take anything seriously, ever. But the main reason is because my idea of gravity differs from the standard that people generally agree on these days. I have my own internal rules about what I think is important, and I have to forego being part of a group if I want to follow those principles. Whereas I would love it if people would fundamentally understand me, I can't make that my highest priority. I have to go out and do a lot of embarrassing unintelligible things, without asking for any feedback or support. It's weird.

So where does one end up, following this interminable road of guilty pleasures and moronic pursuits? Sometimes it's a matter of being completely embarrassed of yourself at all times, but staying on course, unable to get off the train. I have forced myself to make the most mortifying music and perform it with a straight face in front of actual persons a million times. When I hear the lyrics of the songs I wrote, I wince at regular intervals. Yet I keep on acting in the same way, as if I have no shame.

The Worst Women Ever

I hope this doesn't offend anyone, but some types of women are the worst women ever. I have a permanent fixation with examining and emulating the most disgusting ones. One day I hope to be as gross as they are. I strive to observe dames in their natural habitat so I can learn their foul secrets. I can't tell whether I'm doing a good job or not so far, but a few people have called me a vapid cunt at various times, so I must be on the right track.

I was at a fancy restaurant in Hollywood and one of these individuals was seated near me. She was essentially a fine quality piece of ass, and she was on the fast track to getting ahead in life from a professional standpoint. She had this nightmarish high lady voice and she was pronouncing every "s" way too sharply, like the piercing scream of a snake from Hades. She was saying things like "Cheersss", and "I think everyone should take businesss classesss no matter what they do otherwisse". A perfect example of the horror that surrounds us, and I found it riveting.

Some ladies are frequently shrieking and drunk, and they are either too hot or too cold. Their itunes crashed and they need to tell you about it. When they are happy their typing will be a fountain of exclamation points.

What's funny to me is how men view these gals in the world of white people who are going places in the big city. First of all, a woman has to be as thin as possible, and be for all intents and purposes a fancy grade A piece of meat. When men say they are looking for a friendly girl with a great smile, they are leaving out/implying the most important part, which is that the friendship and smile need to be attached to the piece of meat, first and foremost. The dame should not bust your balls or tell you what to do. Intelligence is optional, as long as it doesn't detract from the meat part, (as might happen in the case of a feminist, for example). Now for me in particular, I personally would never appeal to one of these superficial dude guys, primarily because insanity is a big minus, and I am fucking loco. However there was no chance in hell of me getting involved in a relationship of that sort anyway, because those types of men make me gag on sight.

Conformity And How Cool It Is

So everything I do is a study in conformity. It is all a self-conscious, emblematic tribute to what I have been led to believe constitutes –the world-, or –a human life-. Instead of trying to lay out a definitive impression of who I am, or what I ultimately care about, I try to make light of things that appeal to me in the world at large, and joke around and try to send out something that I wouldn't expect from myself. I like to dwell on the lowest common denominators of people in general, to the extent that I'm able to relate.

It's interesting to create something that's an impression of what you think a normal person might do. Try to remove yourself from the equation, if only by fifty percent, and let it be something that doesn't completely remind you of yourself. I think, can a song have an identity entirely independent of the person who created it? Can I go around with a straight face while expressing absurd and infantile sentiments? Can I handle the notion that I may be perceived as absurd and infantile because those qualities are the ones I arbitrarily decided to promote?

Walking away from humanity you get an aesthetic result that is alienated, depressed, and disturbed in nature. It might be valuable in terms of pathos, and might be important to people who are also alienated to begin with. But the life of the nonconformist is always in danger of being extremely painful. If you can't or won't meet people halfway, you're setting yourself up to be alone in a very profound way. If you can't handle widespread contemporary stupidity, you will have a terrible sense of humor and be very bitter!

It's interesting to me because, from critics' perspectives, in the 20th century the idea of conformity in art was only perceived as having negative connotations. The artist, in this view, should be an unprecedented individual attempting to diverge from the status quo and arrive at some novel perspective. The old stereotype was of a disturbed and misunderstood genius. But then a new trend started to evolve which was, what are the limits beyond which you can't consider something "art". For example if Chris Burden shoots himself in an art gallery, that is now considered art, whereas before he did it, it would have been crazy to think that could ever be "art". Nowadays, people are making all sorts of bs and calling it art, which is fine with me. And we don't really know where it will end, I mean, how low is too low? What constitutes "bad taste"? Something as elemental as mainstream media or porn conflicts with all notions of subtlety or esoteric thought. But to be elemental and thereby raw, is that any less representative of the realities of human life? Pandering, garish imagery, and sensational violence, can those be regarded on the same level of honesty as fine art or literature?

The cool thing is: I think that art at this point is so dead, and has been dead for so long, that we can talk about this type of stuff all we want and it won't even matter one shred! We can talk about whether stupid things are art all night long and no one will care! THAT's some postmodern shit right there. We should put THAT on the wall in an art gallery which is really just a coffee store, for people to glance at for one second while they are buying coffee.

Artifice, Fakeness, And Civilization

"The force of civilization is to construct giant glass buildings, over and over forever, every one of them seething with fakeness, a reality imposed on the earth only by our will."

-Me, apparently, wtf

Oh wow I don't remember writing this. It's a pretty strong statement? I agree with it, maybe it seems a little extra angry though. Whoa. Was I trying to go to the poetry zone? Probably not, I was probably just freaking out as usual.

This is interesting though, because since I wrote it, I read an article about the current real estate situation in China, which is very unusual and reminds me of this exact image! Apparently there has been a huge amount of development/construction there which far exceeds the demand for property. There are empty cities being built that are brand new and unoccupied, because they are in bad locations and no one can afford to move in. I saw some scary aerial photographs showing these fancy metro skyscrapers that have no residents, and highways with no cars on them.

When you're a hippie, it's sort of a reflex to think that cities look horrifying and that people would be better off living on farms. I used to have that problem pretty bad. I thought true happiness was available only in forests. Actually it was just a guess, life wasn't going so well for me at that point so it was a stab in the dark. Liberal persons tend to associate human fabrications with being somehow false or a lie. Like the fact that we are surrounded by all these buildings and technology is so unnatural that our souls are being oppressed. But what about the fact that it's amazing and incredible? Think about it, could you yourself personally build a TV or a phone?? We take A LOT of weird things for granted.

To me, what it all proves is that humans are capable of anything. We really have no excuse for thinking there's any idea that would be impossible to create in reality. It's being demonstrated for us every single day. If you have some impossible goal to achieve and you don't know if you'll ever be able to do it, just think about transistors and semiconductors for a little while.

The Reasons Why My Project Interests Me:

1. I enjoy applying discipline and rigor to a genre that is typically approached according to whim, or practiced mainly by goofballs. I don't mean this to sound derisive at all, but it's easier to make foolish self-serving music if you're stupid. That way, you aren't aware of how embarrassing it is. I'm an uptight white person and I hang out with a lot of uptight white people. It doesn't come naturally to me to talk about sex or even to dance in public at a party. I'm the kind of person who, in a public place, just wears a sweater and doesn't talk to you. Not because of rudeness or unfriendliness, but because talking to people is weird. Also I'm completely sober 97% of the time, and when you factor that in, my style makes less and less sense until it makes no sense.

2. After starting initially, I realized it would be much more demanding and complicated that I had assumed. This bizarre impenetrability made the challenge more interesting. One day hopefully

I'll just fall out of bed in the morning and have everything be automatically great, and it'll be really easy. But up to now I would say things have been confusing and tricky, and basically frustrating.

3. I got carried away by processing the concept of primitivism from an extremely subjective viewpoint, that is also uniquely specific to this time in history. I like the elemental nature of human emotions. I am looking for the antidote to the set of aesthetic choices that was presented to me when I was younger, which left me disillusioned and bereft of enjoyment in life. So I like to pick up on and canonize the retardation I see out there, and try to distill and transmute it into a finer form. When I ask myself on the most sincere level what I honestly desire to create, usually what I come up with is that I want to generate a lot of smut. Specifically not smut that is shocking or unusual, but instead has been vaguely sanitized to be acceptable for general audiences.

One of the main tenets of my aesthetic desire is to adopt idiotic forms of expression and assimilate myself into the worst elements of society. I intentionally try to manifest my projects in as dumb a way as possible. This seems to be a difficult point for observers to understand, because why would an adult person in the full light of consciousness make that decision? Is it an attempt to patch together some justification for sub-standard work? People have a huge difficulty separating the creator from the thing they created. How could it be a work of fiction?

The answer is, I like certain things that are dumb. I prefer them. My ability to think clearly, to articulate my thoughts, the validity of my sense of aesthetics, none of these things are on the line. I have nothing to prove to anyone and I don't care what people's impression of me is. I feel entirely justified, even if it seems like I have the worst taste imaginable.

4. Remember to do things for hypothetical people of the future who you may meet. What if you get a lucky break? Make sure you are ready. The future, also, could be in a week, who knows?

Why Are We Alive

Sorry but the world is a huge frightening place. Have people in history ever been bombarded with such a convolution of polarizing information as we are? How does everyone handle it? In order to function I have to absorb the emotional implications of all these nightmarish current events that are thrown at us every day. Maybe I'm being overly sensitive, but I know it's way too much for me personally and I have to block some of it out. Maybe a good strategy is to narrow one's focus to one's immediate subjective circle of experiences, and ignore "the world"? My feelings are too strong and I think I periodically shut down and am unable to act because of it. My instinct is definitely to hide. Are there people out there who are fully processing the giant scope of this influx and their minds aren't exploding? I'm looking for signs of explosion, but it seems that everyone is pretty relaxed. Actually, now that I think about it, no one is having this problem and it must just be me.

Here's the thing: so many fucked up things are going to happen in our lifetime. What am I supposed to do about that? Obviously we can't break down and turn into sobbing piles every time someone dies on the news, which is always. A lot of people deal with it by getting mad and yelling, they yell about the government and public policy and things like that. Maybe that helps them feel better but it doesn't work for me. For myself I really don't have a solution.

I was talking with some people about Foucault, or whatever, and I thought, Foucault is really not helping me out here at all. Because of course you just want someone to walk up to you and hand you the answers to life. Nobody you know ever has any good answers to life, not even your therapist, so if that happened it would be amazing. But not THOSE kinds of answers. Critiques of society's ills are not the answers I personally can use for anything. A detailed account of things sucking, and exactly why they suck, and every possible angle on how precisely they suck is just old news to me. Isn't that type of thinking the first thing a liberal person would arrive at given any amount of introspection? Do people even need to attend a political science class to figure that crap out? These days, doesn't everyone have a little tiny Foucault voice inside them that starts yelling periodically about how wrong the system is? Anyway sorry if I can't be Mr. Answers-To-Life for you, sorry about that!

Moving on: I like how, in this society, there is a total absence of death. No one is allowed to die. And if someone dies, they had better be extremely old or extremely sick. Every death is treated as a bizarre anomaly that could have been prevented and should be thoroughly examined.

I used to spend a lot of time watching old movies from WWII, and when you do that you can tell there was not always a no-deaths-allowed policy. People have been dying like crazy since the beginning of civilization! I know it's hard to believe, but even in the last 100 years it was like that. Now when we read about violence and wars overseas, we think it must be unique to other continents. We think unconsciously, if these countries would hurry up and develop a zero tolerance choose-life agenda, things could get a lot better for all their residents. Which is rude of us.

Anyway, it's great for me because as long as no one is going to die, then I feel like I'm totally safe and I can go about my business with a spring in my step. It really boosts my confidence while driving and running errands.

The no-death policy is probably the coolest feature of Western Civilization, aside from indoor plumbing. Why don't people celebrate indoor plumbing more often? Everyone, this is cause for a celebration! Indoor plumbing is a really really big deal to me and I think if you spend more time thinking about it, you'll feel the relevance in your own life.

Do You Want To Hear About How Depressed I Am?

This is the part of the book where I think, what is the best thing to put into a book? I want to take a little moment and say I don't know! Why should anyone know? Why couldn't there be a blank page sometimes, to represent the time when the author didn't have a goddamn answer for you? Let's have a blank page just for fun though...

.

.

.

.

.

.

.

.

.

.

.

.

.

.

.

.

.

.

.

.

.

.

.

Was that fun or what?!

The weird time or interval between inspirations, what can you say about it? You know that you have had good ideas in the past and worked on them. You can feel that you will have good ideas in the future, but you can't force them to occur now. You want to work on something that you care about, but there is no immediate answer. You can't fake your way through it. There's not much going on!

I don't like lying there trying to think, but it happens all the time. It's much better to be consumed by something that's already in your mind. Sometimes all you have is a small idea, or a piece of an idea, or the memory of an idea you had weeks or months ago. But no matter how faint of a shred it is, you have to hold on to it, because some other times you've got nothing, and you're lying there for 4 hours wondering what to do next! That for me is the worst, being in a complete stasis, unable to move forward, with no info coming in.

It's difficult to stay on a stable schedule. Some days I have elaborate plans to complete earth-shattering projects, one immeasurably huge step at a time. Other days I plan to eat a lot and then bleed out of my crotch. It's always a toss-up.

When I have a phase like that it's like I'm barely even alive. I'll stay home for days designing or programming something and wandering around trying to think. I probably end up getting a lot of work done at those times, but I won't go outside or see people or talk to anyone for a long stretch. I can't tell if it's good or bad, but maybe it's the only way I can get enough space to do any critical thinking? When life moves fast I feel better and I enjoy myself more, but would I ever work on anything worthwhile? It's hard to say.

Maybe it's a good thing to go into one of those total sensory deprivation holes, maybe I should value that state more? Could it be a really beneficial way to spend time in terms of progress? That would be great for me, because it happens to me so often. Generally the stasis is so heavy though, that I want it to end as soon as possible!

Some projects just take me so long it's unbelievable. It makes me wonder what the hell I do all day, even though I am there with me the whole time. I think, it can't be right, it can't be this hard to accomplish something. I wonder how the world functions, since I still can't get it together, even though I have so much free time! People must be absolute wizards.

But then, every time I make anything, as soon as it's done I completely forget all the work that went into it. It's as if it just fell out of the sky and I had nothing to do with it. I forget all the screw-ups, and days and days of sitting there saying wtf to myself, when I don't have the answer yet or any remote clue.

What I Think About Music

I have to go out on a limb and try to explain an idea that I think people will not be receptive to. I think that no matter how well I describe it, it will sound contentious and unfair and no one will get it. It's something I've noticed empirically in my experiences and thought about a lot though. So before rejecting the theory, allow me to elaborate somewhat.

Everyone listens to music for emotional purposes. Most assume that the music merely echoes a feeling they already had inside. But is it possible that music could "brainwash" a person with its inherent panel of feelings? Is it possible that listening to sad, slow, or whimsical songs could make me feel worse afterwards?

First of all, depression is not an on-off switch. It's a spectrum with different levels of severity. A lot of people would never characterize themselves as depressed, but it's obvious that they are on the borderline, and they are not entirely healthy at all. These are the people for whom bummer music is made. When you're scraping by and things are just mildly ok, that's a shade of depression, which will cause you to respond favorably to those types of genres. You would say, this isn't a "downer," you would find it to be "uplifting", "transformative", and "spiritual". But I contend, that music will sound good to you only when you're down. When you feel actually good and your health is great and you love your life, you could absolutely leave all of those preferences behind.

Identifying with painful music is a survival mechanism for rough times, I think. Case in point: who listens to the most depressing music, stereotypically? Answer: disturbed teenagers. I'm only saying this because I've noticed it myself, that my taste in music changes alongside changes in my state of mental health. I pay attention to my feelings because I'm always looking to keep away from the dark side.

So then my next thought is that maybe by producing music that has more inherent energy and more (for lack of a better word) positivity, it could actually facilitate better health in the listener. That would be great if it were true. I could also extrapolate that we should coerce ourselves to listen to happier music since that would be in our best interest over time. But I don't want to do that, because it sounds sort of fascist to me.

The truth is, I actually listen to very little music. I'll fixate on a few songs and be obsessed with them, and discard everything else because it doesn't do much for me. A lot of the time I am convinced that music as an entity fucking sucks in its entirety. But I know that's not true. I think I just get sick of it, I get burned out from trying to do production all day. Sometimes I forget what music even IS, and I think – why would anybody like that garbage? I get confused! I've just spent too many hours sitting there when I'm trying to create something, deliberating over a thousand miniature parameters, to have a sensible perspective anymore.

I have a cool ability to not hear music if it doesn't sound interesting to me. It's the same as if you could turn off the sound of a car alarm or a police siren in your mind. It could be a live band or a recording, it doesn't even matter. If it sucks to me, then my brain switches off automatically and I'll think about something else. For example, I'm not partial to rock these days, so rock music I absolutely don't even hear. It's out of my life and I'm so happy it's gone. I can't tell you what it means to me that I can universally reject these unnecessary things.

This skill backfires all the time though, because then I won't know what something sounds like, even if I've heard it multiple times. A lot of enthusiasts like to hear and know about every band and every project out there, just to have an encyclopedic knowledge of what musicians are up to in the world. But I'll never be able to pull that off because I reject unappealing audio instantaneously.

I enjoy hanging out with people who make music. They really don't seem to care about anything, in a good way. It's charming because it's as if they have no respect even for their own lives! Throwing your life away to do something stupid is a great feeling.

The best people are the ones who make music so artsy or bizarre that they can't expect to ever make a living off of it. The absurdity of being in that position in life really contributes to one's character. The future is like an open book, you know that some series of stupid events will occur that you will enjoy, and that's about it. You know that your friends will appreciate whatever you make, and maybe some other people, but it doesn't matter very much.

There's a sense of cameraderie that develops between people who have the same taste in music. It is a very small group of people so they stick together. Some music just sounds so subtle, or alternately so repellent, that it's never going to appeal to a very big audience. And some music is meant to be performed live, so only people who actually show up for the performance will really understand it.

Writing music feels like a bad habit sometimes. It becomes easier and more gratifying to write music all day than to go outside and do other things. It's a good hiding place where real life can't get a hold of you. A lot of times I have to force myself not to go back and work on production because it's such a default. The awful part is that it's all circuitous, anything you compose could sound ok, you could drift away forever, without getting any interesting results. Even talking about it this way, I realize how raunchy the topic is. Music is bad and gross!

Hey Naomi, I'm the same as you! I sit all day too and work on songs I'm writing. Yeah well the difference is, I know how incredibly nasty that practice is, and you still think it's neat and cool. What bothers me is the aimlessness of it all, guys wienering around congratulating themselves about the power of their own creations.

Living In A Fantasy World

Here's the thing about living in a fantasy world and getting everything you want. You get acclimated to it immediately and completely take it for granted. A person will always feel entitled to everything they have if not more. It's pretty gross. There is sort of a vague awareness that some other people out there might not have the same opportunity, but it doesn't affect your view of them and you never really think about it.

No matter how well things are going for you though, everyone still has to go through the same first-world-white-person quotidian asshole problems. For example your coffee might not be the exact way you wanted it, or you might lose your phone. Maybe there are people somewhere who are living entirely in a cloud, and they are non-mortal and untouchable, but probably they still get just as steamed when their helicopter pilot doesn't show up on time to take them down to the waterfall.

Some people are definitely happier than others though. You know when you ask someone how they're doing and they immediately say "GREAT" and they think life is way too fantastic. They always have a lot of force in their tone because they are so amped about every goddamn day. Do those people annoy you? They think regular shit is a miracle. You could hear them talking about a bar for example, a regular nice bar where you could go and have an ok time. And they would say what a –miracle- time they had there, and how –amazing- it was, and how their one friend was there who is an –amazing- person. It makes you delve into the far reaches of your mind trying to imagine having such an awesome time, and thinking about how that girl didn't amaze you that bad, and you can't exactly figure out how they did it, and you consider the possibility that drugs may be involved?

For me, I've been really lucky in that I've been able to devote the last few years to projects I care the most about, but I forget how unusual that is constantly. If something good happens in my life I try to forget about it, because I think if I start to congratulate myself then I'll never get any work done. I'm more interested in trying to focus on my problems so that then maybe they are more likely to get solved. I try to stay pretty neutral. I guess that means I'm uptight and I'll never have a good life! I think I'll be happy enough if I can manage to accomplish something every day, even if it's a thing that other humans will never know about or appreciate.

The bottom line is though, that you really should be living in a fantasy world even if you won't appreciate half of it. Reality is too real and it takes up 23 hours of your day if you're not careful. It's better to create an independent situation for yourself, a separate place you can live in instead, strung together with diversions and ephemera. Don't let regular life push you around. Be the boss, you know? Success to me means being able to transcend reality and spend lots of time as if in a waking dream. I feel sometimes that I have exited the world, in a good way.

Your mind should be like a private exclusive club that no one can get into, except maybe your cat.

Telling Yourself You Suck – For Success

The list of things I would congratulate myself for, in terms of life goals, is very limited and short. When people feel too cool about their accomplishments I find it a very embarrassing state of being. It's honestly one of the least attractive traits I think a person could have. I find it much better to dismiss and ignore your own track record, even if you are doing the right thing. All you amount to is the result of the work you've done every single day to haul ass and be your best, so if you sit back and accept whatever victories you might have accrued, that's when you begin to crumble into some decayed jerk-off. I know that sounds hyperbolic but I see people do it all the time.

However, I want to also say that it's 100% a separate situation when dealing with the minutia of day to day life. I feel infinite pride for taking a shower and having sort of a clean desk. It's a stroke of absolute genius when you can say to yourself, wow, I really closed that window at the exactly correct moment before it started to get cold outside. And I don't even want to get started talking about stellar parking spaces and the way they can lift your spirits to the sky. I know, it's a double standard.

Every once in a while when I go out, acquaintances will start to get excited about me, and tell me how cool they think I am, and they'll want me to have a conversation about my videos or something. That is too weird for me and it makes me feel uncomfortable. When someone thinks you're too cool, they want to talk to you about YOU, and that's weird. In regular life you would say "Hey! Let's talk about worms and rocks!" And then you would talk about worms and rocks as two anonymous interested parties. After a long day of being alive, who would want to be forced to continue focusing on one's perpetually rotten self?

I would much rather be disregarded as some sort of fixture by the people around me than marveled at or something. How embarrassing is it to register on someone's radar as being "important"? As long as I'm not lurking around to the point where it seems like I need to be told to go home, it's much better to just leave me in the corner and not make a big deal out of it.

There is one good thing about people telling you you're great though. The good part of receiving a compliment is, that you can maybe spend 10 less minutes per day troubleshooting.

Sometimes you start to get a little down though, and then that's when you need to give yourself a revitalizing pep talk. You have to say whatever you can to get motivated again. Here are a few things you could tell yourself in the event that life was not looking as good as it should:

You are the greatest person alive today, including Steven Hawking and five dollar footlongs.

Your directorial debut in the 80s was acclaimed by the critics, and was a box office financial sensation.

Your smile is used on nights and weekends by lighthouses in the area, to send out a shiny beacon to ships lost at sea.

You will run a marathon and win by such a huge margin, that you'll have time to use the bathroom on the track and not have to pee on yourself while you're running.

Not Giving Up - So Many Times In A Row

Here's the thing, it's always been common wisdom that you're not supposed to quit or give up on your dreams. It's easy to say "never give up". But what I think is being glossed over here is the extreme amount of times you have to not give up. I mean you literally have to not give up so many times in a row, and then life sneaks around the back way and tries to make you give up in all these obscure new ways. You really have to be on your toes. You even have to consider, you could be giving up and not knowing it!

I try really hard not to quit or be a quitter. I feel like that strategy is possibly working, but it's hard to say for sure. Every single day it seems like I hit some sort of wall and then decide to quit and then have to regroup and do all the same work I had planned to do anyway. But sometimes quitting masquerades as a rational solution to your problems. Sometimes giving up is the only logical answer you can come up with, and it makes sense, and then you have to talk yourself down and keep going regardless. I'm always scraping my way forward through time, one particle at a time, and it's so dumb.

But I think that if I keep going, I could build an entire empire based only on sheer foolishness, and I can't resist that idea. When you start to see evidence in real life of the magnitude of amazing garbage you can create out of absolute nowhere, you think, why would anyone ever choose to default to regular life instead?

This is especially true if you decide to use your life to make weird music. Having the balls to consciously spend your time that way and not quit is pretty funny. Unless you're an idiot, you're going to have to sit down with yourself at some point and say: look, this is what I'm doing right now. There's not going to be any logic to it, but just don't worry about that and don't give me a hard time. It's going to be stupid. Just don't concentrate on that aspect of it, or start going around considering alternate career options.

I used to get all fussy and worried all the time about the future and whether things would turn out ok for myself and the world. I still could, I could worry about that right this second, if you want me to. I could get loco about forty different queries and spend the rest of the day blinking in disillusionment, any day of the week. See you there!

But recently I've got a sports strategy that is doing a lot to keep me excited, so I don't waste all my time thinking about the stupid garbage of tomorrow. Although I have to say, I'm not into sports generally. I'm sorry but I find them all boring. Unless you count professional poker tournaments as a sport. That's the only one I like.

The thing I do like about sports is how you're supposed to constantly be revved up at all times, and talk yourself up to victory, and trick your brain into being disciplined and staying on target. So anyway what I've been telling myself lately is that all you have to do is "hit a home run" every single day, and that after a while, all those days will add up, and your result will be a lot of momentum/success. Writing the words "hit a home run" was pretty embarrassing for me just now, I didn't anticipate that! I mean it sounds stupid, but I believe that it's true. I think you have to keep coming back every day and take a piece out of life, and make it as epic as you can.

See right now, nobody would want to take that advice from me, but one day when I'm "the Steve Jobs of being alive", i.e. incredible, then all kinds of middle management types are going to be throwing my wisdom around. They'll say to their teams "Naomi got to where she's at by hitting a home run every day", and then all the employees will nod to themselves and resolve to hit home runs.

I Am A Cripple

I am really really into taking care of my
health, because the fact of the matter is, my health
sucks a big dick and it has for years and years. I
don't even want to go into all the stupid physical
malfunctions I've been dealing with, because it's
such an inordinate amount! I know it's rude of me
to say this, but I essentially consider myself a
cripple. Is that even a word anymore? It sounds
like an archaic slur, like Oriental!

If this were the 19th century, I would have
already died from consumption. Maybe I could
even have been an infant mortality. I would have
been the little baby grave in the front yard. 1801-
1801, what a cutie. Ideally my parents would have
had a portrait painted of me in advance, to
commemorate my existence. If I ever end up
getting an abortion, I should probably have a
portrait painted of the pregnancy test that came
out positive. It's important to have respect for
new life, you know? Maybe it would be enough

just to have a photo of myself holding the pregnancy test, looking sad.

Things got really out of control with the tuberculosis though back in the old days. Even though people were dying these slow, horrible, mysterious deaths, TB started to adopt its own creative romantic style. It started to be glamorous for women to waste away and die, and it made them much more attractive, which you can read about in stories like La Boheme and Wuthering Heights etc. It made for a good story because it would take them forever to die, maybe years, and they would lose a lot of weight and get very pale, which was probably a bonus. They wore those giant lacy nightshirts the whole time, they were bedridden, they would faint, they would have good days and bad days, and doctors didn't know what the hell was going on. Actually the medical community was able to add to the mystique, by having no idea what the disease even was. They just called it consumption, or even "the disease".

Anyways, I'm on this awful restricted diet where I can't even have bread, I have to exercise for an hour every day, and there are about 40 vitamins I have to take or I will basically drop dead. But I'm not high maintenance or anything. I can barely drink alcohol and I can't smoke or do drugs. I would never complain though because I feel good, and before I knew how to do all those things I felt like ass at all times and I was a wreck.

It's weird being addicted to vitamins. I always have millions of vitamins in my bag. I get worried that in an emergency I would be separated from my vitamins. I'm also addicted to sun protection, specifically sunscreen and hats. I feel like everyone should have a lot of hats on them, available at all times. In southern California that's not too weird of a concept, since the sun is out to radiate you 24/7 and it doesn't take breaks.

It's fine, we're all going to die from MSRA anyway, I'm chill with that.

Cooking Tips: Never Cook Again!

Do you love food? Think about it. The
world is replete with incredible snacks. There are
delicious products raging around every corner.
However, Baby is on a restricted diet and Baby
can only eat the most special and rare of the many
snacks. That is to say, boring and stupid health
food for hippies. Sucks to be me!

But seriously, actually, don't listen to
anything I say about food. I eat the weirdest crap
ever. My goals are to be 1) gluten free, 2) organic
whenever possible, and 3) stick to minimal
preparation time/effort. When you draw up a
venn diagram and intersect all those concepts, the
results are not going to be delicious. Sometimes it
works out, and I'll be drinking a quart of
unpasteurized tangerine juice while I'm driving on
the freeway. Those are the good times. Also I
might get the five-dollar caviar from the Japanese

market and eat that while I'm reading blogs.

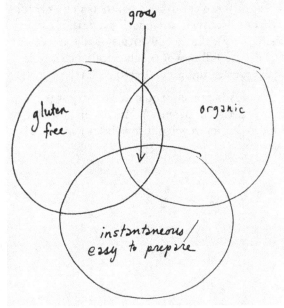

gross

gluten
free

organic

instantaneous /
easy to prepare

But usually I'll throw together something weird that no one would ever eat. I started spraying my toast with spray oil. Yes I am the asshole who invented that. What is wrong with me?

But what about an energy bar? You could eat one of those. Mmmmmmmm. Those are good! All you have to do is buy them and your job is done!

Also you could get frozen yogurt: how is it that men can eat frozen yogurt? Isn't it only for women? I see men eating it all the time, it's so weird. Isn't it the most womany of all the foods? I feel like it's full of woman chemicals, like it will make you cry and watch Bravo on TV.

Additionally, you could go stay at your mom's house. A parent's house is a great source of food. Your mom will put strawberries in a bowl for you.

An Essay: Detractors Solely Degrade Themselves

Here's a little essay I wrote when I first realized how rude and unfriendly some people treat each other on the Internet. It's really cold and dry, because I was fed up with how poorly these people had thought the situation through. They thought they were anonymous, but I could see everything about them, and it didn't appeal to me!

A person leading an interesting life doesn't have time to fume about the innocuous deeds of others, especially of strangers.

A person leading a happy life has no inclination to promote hate or negativity, unless it's in the interest of an altruistic cause, such as indemnifying those who would commit crimes against humans or the environment.

Therefore, if detractors seek to disparage a peer or a public figure, they are effectively proclaiming themselves to be sad losers.

There is an element of envy exposed as well, because the aggressor is stuck at home, lonely and isolated, while the object of hate is out and about, living a life of normal or above-normal momentum.

In this society, it is not looked on as favorable to be lonely, fat, and sad. Why would anyone voluntarily mark himself or herself as part of that demographic?

If you happen to say something bad about someone via the Internet, it reflects directly, immediately back on you.

Is there anything more embarrassing than a bitter, bored person, who contributes little to nothing to the collective state of humanity, except for trying to criticize the talents of some entertainment figure? Are the skills of the public figure called into question in any way? No: the only thing that's highlighted is the fact that this person has nothing better to do with their time.

These unfortunate casualties were predicted from the very outset of the Internet. The only solution, it seems, would be for each individual to try to enjoy the benefits of going outside, interacting with people in real life, and doing some basic introspection.

And if you happen to become aware of any of these souls plagued by ineffectual anger, take it as an opportunity to smile. Remember your true friends, that your life is unencumbered by Internet addiction, that you're free to create anything you want. Be grateful that you don't have that problem.

In my life, I've met a lot of trolls. I don't know if they ever get better. I consider it a relatively new mental health condition that should one day be chronicled by the medical community. All I can say is, and this is based on my direct experiences, is that it's no way to live.

This is why I can't believe there are still people out there making fun of me on the Internet. Being an Internet joker is so 2006. Back then the Internet was huge and it was the whole world. Now we realize that in fact the world is actually very big and the Internet is only a small fraction of it! So, being a troll in this day and age labels you as a dated casualty of another time, and you become officially "one of those people". So if you're out there typing "So & So is so dumb, they can't do anything" you're essentially wearing a giant shirt that says "I'm a used-up byproduct of the worst case scenario of the Internet, THAT WAS PREDICTED UPON ITS FIRST CONCEPTION! " The worst case scenario being of course that people would become lonely and socially isolated by reducing their level of real life human interaction. I don't get why anyone would want to admit that! Face it guys, lol cats was the hallmark of your generation. Even if you have managed to author an incredible meme, will you ever see any credit for your work? THAT's what you should really be putting more effort into.

If you want to use computers correctly, then go out and find a way to invent a laptop that has a cassette deck built into it. Then I will be impressed by you. (At the time of this writing, it hasn't been done yet to my knowledge.)

Being Addicted To The Internet

First of all, it could happen to anyone, and it sort of comes and goes. I used to be really addicted to the Internet, and as of right now predominantly I'm not, or less so, I hope. I always want to send a message to people who can't get offline that we really are in the midst of an illness! To be honest, I still have all of the symptoms. I check my facebook account periodically all day long, to see what my friends have been doing recently (the last 2 hours). Then I go and read a lot of tech blogs and science periodicals and entertainment news. I like to read while I'm eating, so I try to limit the amount of worthless articles to the duration of snack times. When I'm done snacking then I tell myself it's over. One thing I refuse to do though is hang out in forums. The only people I talk with online are people who I've met in real life, who care about me, and who I consider friends. I think message boards and commenting on random posts can often breed depressing times. Certain demographics I consider to be bad company, in that they can negatively affect your outlook on life.

I became susceptible to the disease at a time when my social life was substandard or maybe just straight-up bad. The bottom line was that I was very isolated and in retrospect, that's not a reality that should be furthered in any way, for anyone. Being online and hanging out in forums all day is a symptom of not having one's life put together well enough. The conversations are not so riveting as you imagine them to be. The lifelong friends that you have made there, largely don't care about you and would probably just as soon watch you get hit by a bus, so they would have something to write about! I have met so many bitter types who were bored, down on themselves, bullying each other, and contributing worthless dialogue that was not helpful to anyone. Of course some people were genuinely funny and delightful, but those people became real friends and separated themselves from the rest pretty quickly. This happened to me in several different communities that I was a part of, so I know it happens as a factor of group dynamics, and wasn't particular to the individuals themselves.

One thing that IS really special is the sociological fascination I have with conversations that are based solely in text. You can't get that in real life. Watching people talk online is the most interesting thing ever. When that was first presented to me, I lost my mind a little bit. Having every artifact of a recent dialogue between two humans, and then reading that as a remote party at a separate third location, is something maybe I'll never get over. Well maybe in a year.

The End - My Masterpizza

Well there you go, that concludes my book. I hope you enjoyed it. I had a great time making it, and I learned a lot as well. For example I learned that nowadays we have the technology to write books while simultaneously browsing the Internet. That one time when I used a quote from Max Headroom, I just cut and pasted all that from some website! I didn't know writing a book could be so easy, I thought it would all be on typewriters! Also I learned that writing isn't so strange, at the end of the day it's a lot like thinking, except your hands get tired after a while.

The difference between writing a book and not writing a book is much bigger than I thought. I'm starting to feel very cool that I went for it. I'm so excited already and no one has even proof-read it yet!